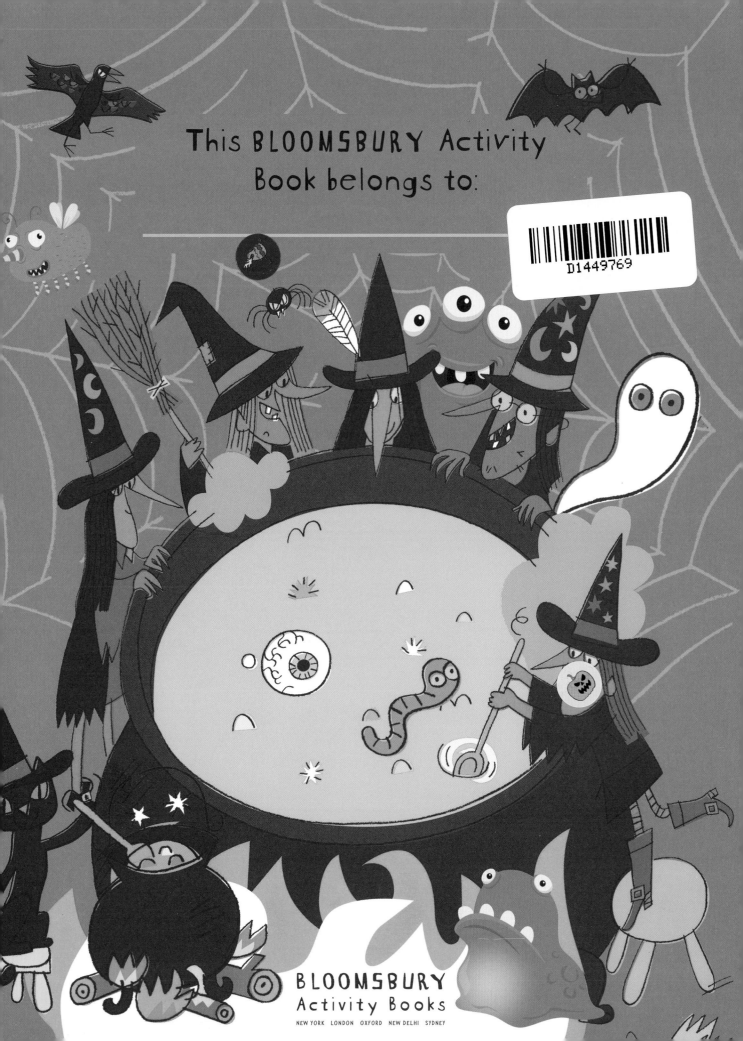

This BLOOMSBURY Activity
Book belongs to:

D1449769

BLOOMSBURY
Activity Books
NEW YORK LONDON OXFORD NEW DELHI SYDNEY

Monster menu! Doodle food that monsters

like to eat.

Write a story about
a monster from space.

Draw the space
monster here.

Which monster spider
can get to the fly
through the maze?

6

Only one shadow matches the witch. Can you find it?

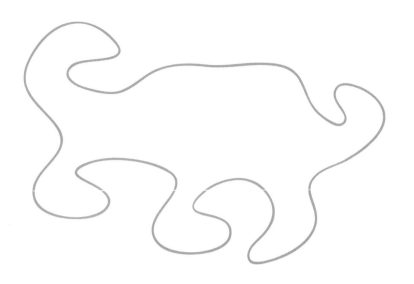

Can you turn the blobs
on this page into monsters?
Add faces, arms, and legs.

9

the witch's clothesline.

Draw an alien in the spaceship.

12

Draw some monsters on the moon.

Turn these vegetables into monsters!

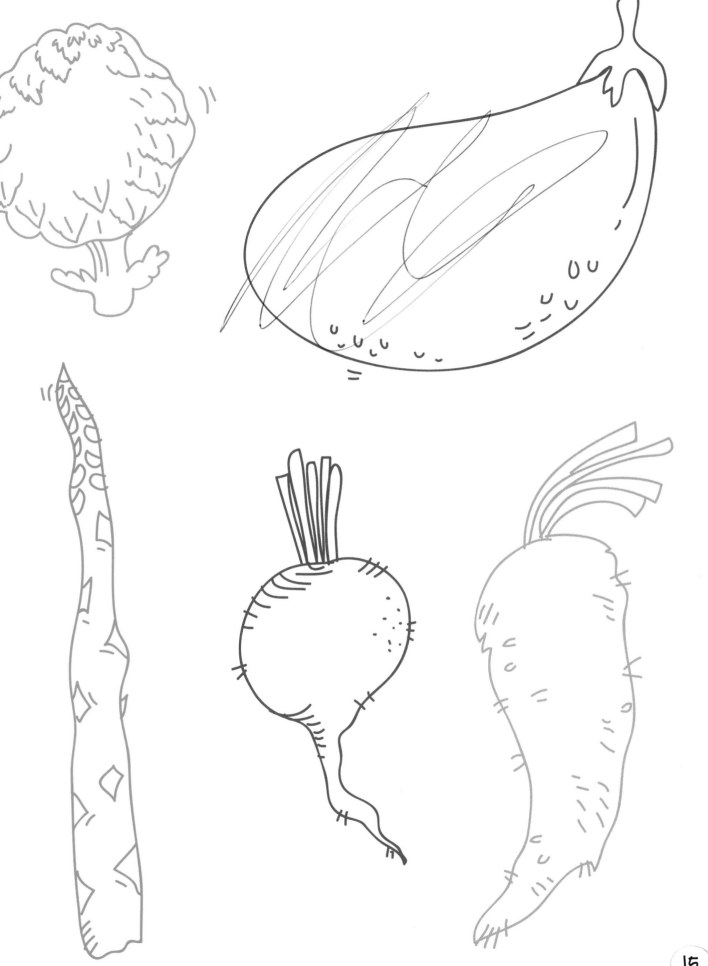

Use the code on this page to write
a spooky message on the opposite page.

Potion name:

Spell:

Contains:

Tastes like:

Potion name:

Spell:

Contains:

Tastes like:

Potion name:

Spell:

Contains:

Tastes like:

Potion name:

Spell:

Contains:

Tastes like:

monster potions.

Potion name:

Spell:

Contains:

Tastes like:

Potion name:

Spell:

Contains:

Tastes like:

Potion name:

Spell:

Contains:

Tastes like:

Potion name:

Spell:

Contains:

Tastes like:

Doodle more monsters wearing parachutes.

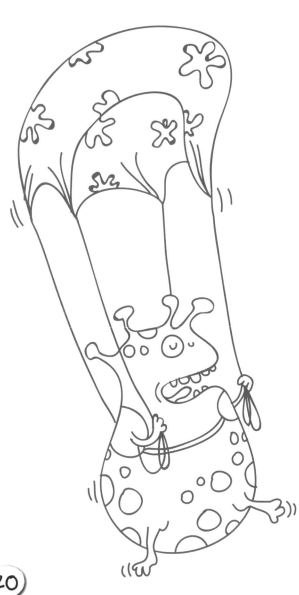

21

Color in the monsters' spaceships.

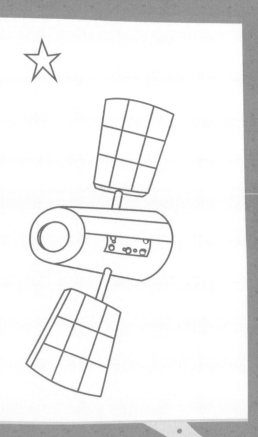

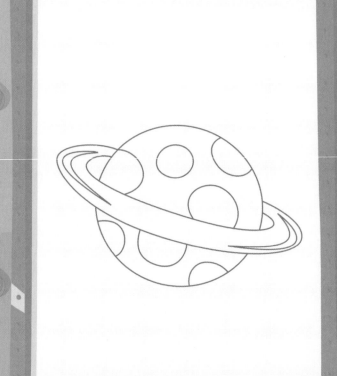

Doodle some creatures
hidden in the snowstorm.

Doodle the bodies of these monsters.

Can you find 4 owls, 5 broomsticks,

and 1 cauldron in this picture?

Draw the monster that lives in this cave.

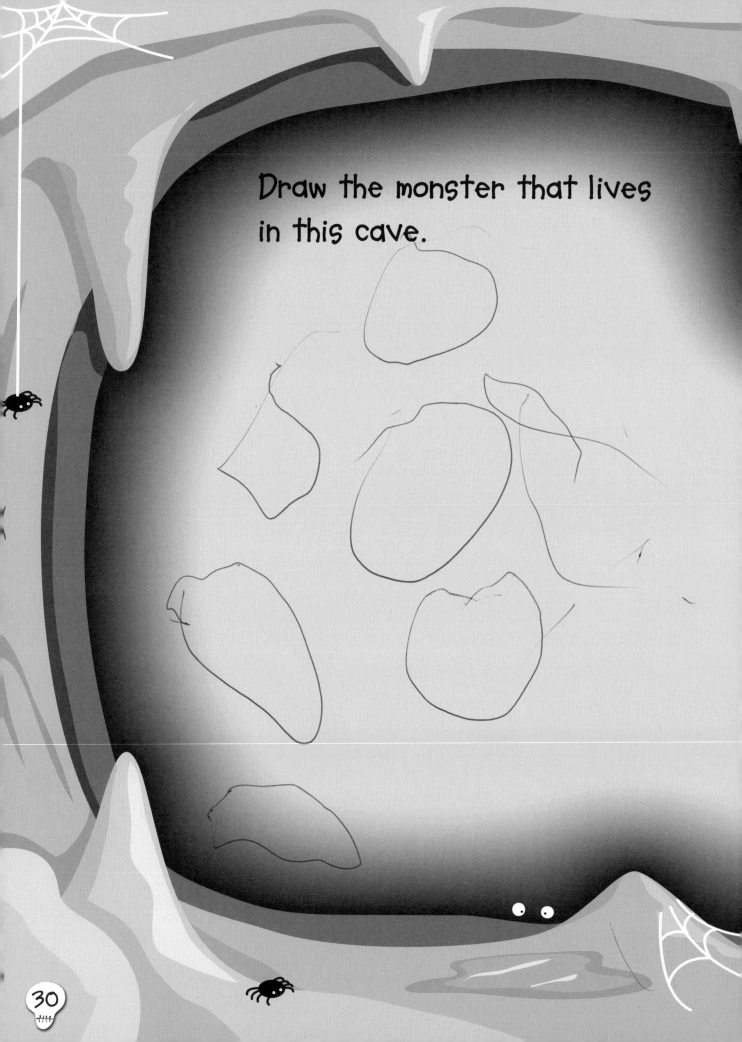

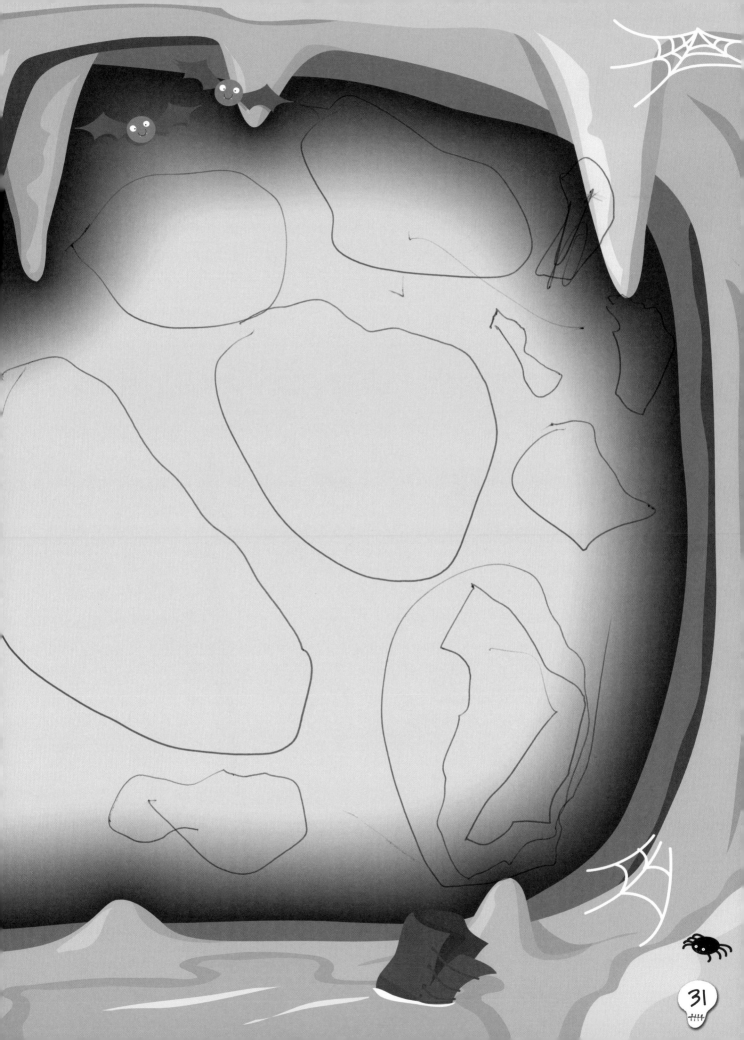

Doodle some more monster bugs in the garden.

Draw a monster robot in each frame.

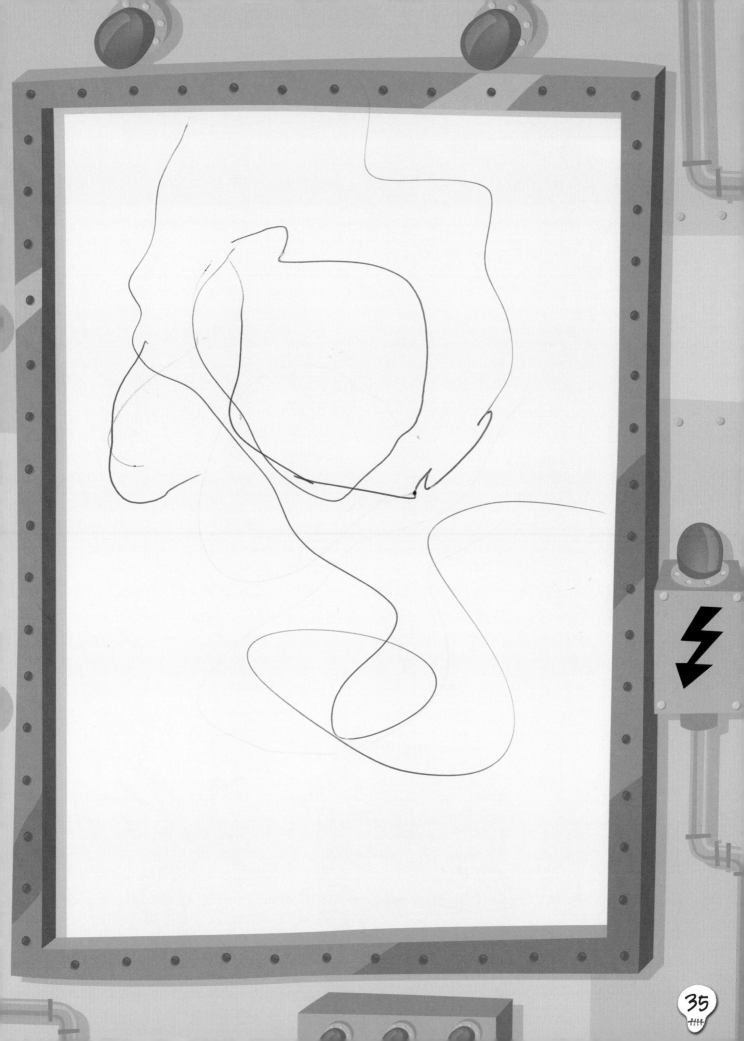

Draw some monster shadows in the

background.

Draw witches under the hats.

Doodle the monsters who have these footprints.

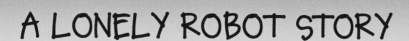

A LONELY ROBOT STORY

Out in space, on a tiny distant planet, there lived a robot.

People had brought the robot to the planet a long time ago, when it was bright and shiny and new. It was a very useful robot. But one day it broke. And when the people got into their rocket to go home, they didn't take the broken robot with them.

So the robot sat on the planet all alone for a long time, with nothing to do.

One day, the robot heard a rumble and a screech. It looked up and saw a spaceship in the sky. The spaceship fell to the ground with a whoosh and a crash. Its door opened, and out came a slimy green alien.

The alien looked at its spaceship and began to cry with all its three eyes. "Oh no!" it sobbed.

The robot was sorry for the alien. "What's wrong?" it asked in its metallic voice.

"My spaceship is broken, so I will be stuck on this planet forever," said the alien. "I can't fix spaceships!"

"I'm a spaceship-fixing robot," said the robot. "My job is fixing spaceships. But I broke and nobody fixed me."

"I'm a robot-fixing alien," said the alien.
"If I repair you, will you fix my spaceship?"

"Yes!" said the robot.

"And will you travel with me in case I crash again?"

"Yes, please!" said the robot.

So the alien fixed the robot, and then the robot fixed the spaceship, and they flew off into space.

Write your own story about a lonely robot.

Doodle more monster laundry on the clothesline.

Draw silly shoes, boots, and hats on the witches.

Z z z

Draw monsters in this creepy landscape

Draw a fire-breathing monster.

Spot the differences
between the two castles.

There are 8 to find.

Draw monster bodies to match the eyes.

56

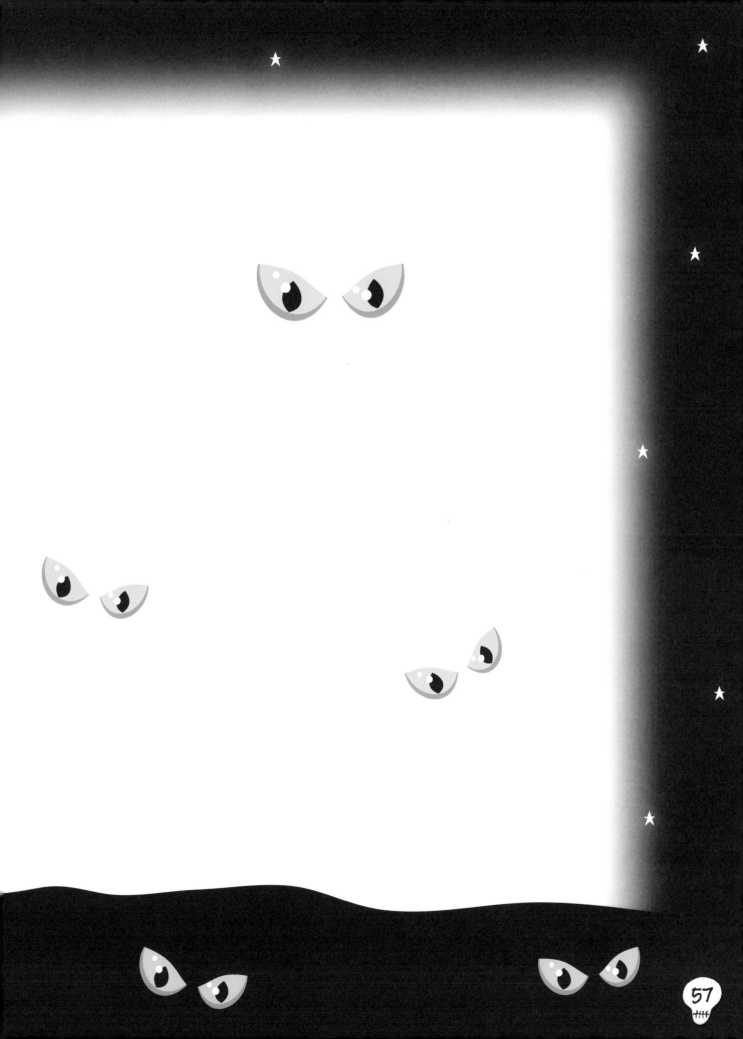

The sad spooky owl needs a friend.
Doodle another tree and owl on the page.

Draw your own
monster faces
on the pumpkins.

Find the matching creepy things.

Using the grid as a guide, copy and color
the scary mummy on the opposite page.

Doodle more scary things on this page.

Follow the lines to see which present
the owls are taking to the party.

Draw a haunted house in the middle of the forest.

Add glasses to
all the monsters'
faces on this
page.

Doodle more monsters in glasses.

Draw lots of yucky things
in the witches' cauldron.

Write something the monster wants to say.

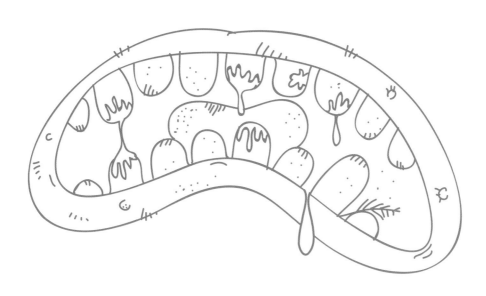

Draw the rest of the monster's face.

YOUR MONSTER PET

First, find a monster. Monsters are hard to spot, so you will have to look carefully for one. A haunted house or a spooky cave could be a good place to start. Look for gigantic footprints or hairy claw marks. Maybe you will see a heap of chewed bones. That makes it easy!

When you have spotted your monster, get a home ready for it. You will need to build big, thick walls so the monster can't escape. Ask a grown-up to help you with the drill. Dig a ditch around your monster house to keep your pet from getting out!

Once your monster house is ready, think about how to catch your new pet. If it's a fast little monster like a bird, you can use a net. A big hairy monster might need handcuffs. Maybe you could lure the monster to a trap with some yummy treats. Bring a bag of eyes.

Don't forget to check with your parents before you bring a pet monster home. Some people don't like creepy, slithery beasts that leave slime on the carpet, or scary, furry things that howl in the night. Grown-ups are very fussy.

And one last rule. Even if your monster is a nice little one that fits easily in a backpack, DON'T BRING IT TO SCHOOL! You'll only get in trouble when it eats the teacher.

Story by Kate Paice

Write your own story about a monster pet.

Who are the monsters trying to frighten?
Draw somebody who looks scared.

ARRHH!

Spot the odd one out
in each group.

WANTED

Draw 2 monster "wanted" posters.

You can use stickers to decorate.

Doodle more monsters with wings.

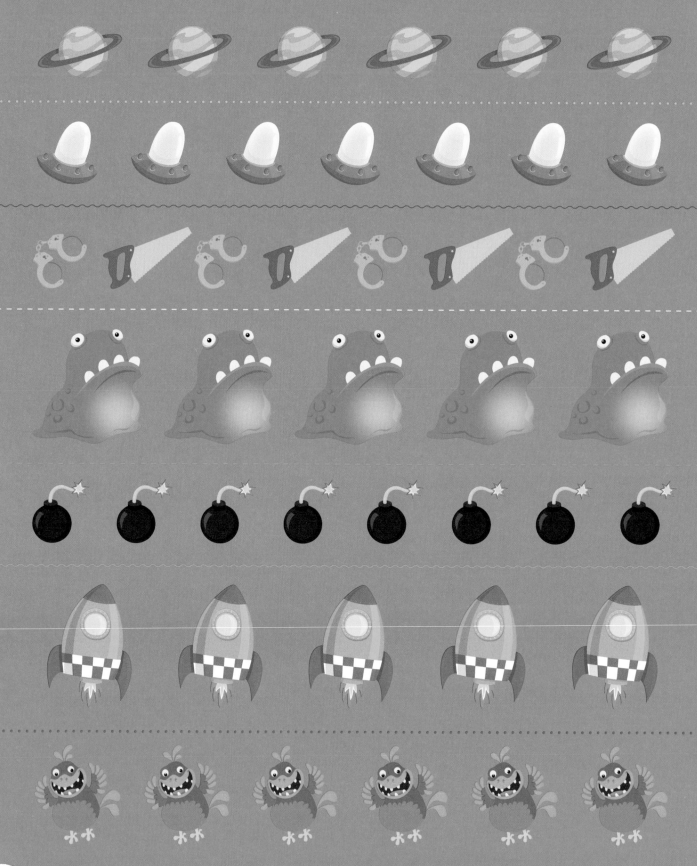

Color the patterns to match the other side.

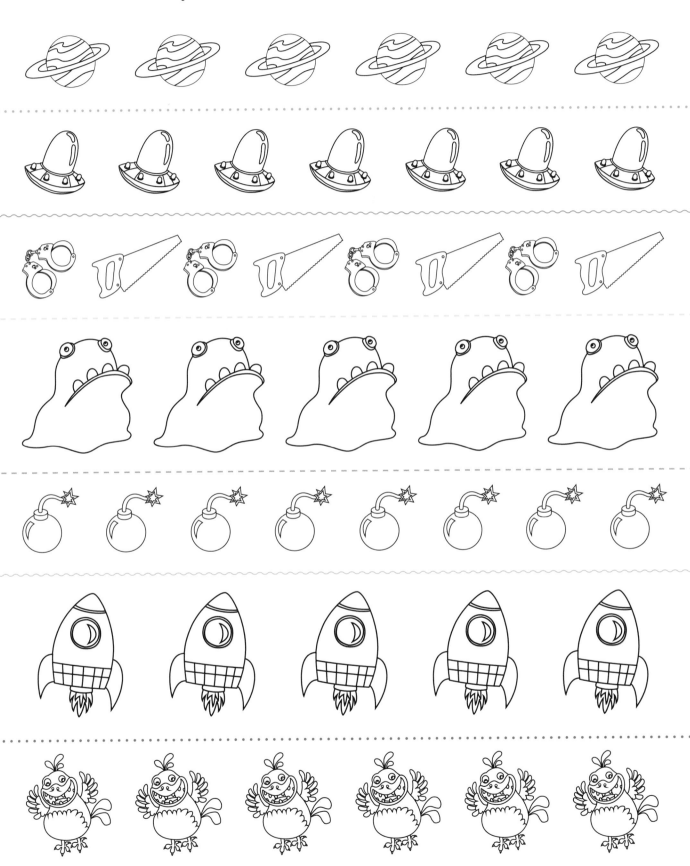

Finish drawing and coloring
the missing scary owls.

89

ROOAAAARR!!

Draw a big space rocket full of aliens.

Draw some monsters
having a party.

Doodle more dancing hairy monsters.

Doodle horns and tails on the cats and dogs.

Trace over the outline and color in the robot.

Can you spot the vampire?

Count the cats, bats, and spiders.
Add sticker eyes to the page.

Doodle more aliens and monsters.

Draw the creatures hiding in the attic.

Design your own monster T-shirts.

Decorate the
T-shirts on
this page
with stickers.

111

Use stickers to fill the jars with spooky ingredients.